# LONG DISTANCE GRANDPARENTING

## A Practical Guide to Building Close Relationships with Your Grandchildren

**Rose Marie Barhydt**
**Bonnie Potter**

Blanfield Publishing, Ann Arbor, MI
Copyright© 1994 by R.M. Barhydt and B. Potter
Published by Blanfield Publishers, Ann Arbor, MI
Printed in United States of America

ISBN  0-9638921-1-8

# LONG DISTANCE GRANDPARENTING

## A Practical Guide to Building Close Relationships with Your Grandchildren

### Rose Marie Barhydt
### Bonnie Potter

Illustrations by:
**Ben Crane**

Layout by:
**Jim Potter**

# Acknowledgements

Special thanks to our wonderful families: Glenn Potter, David Barhydt and Judy Matz, Lisa Barhydt, Lind and Craig Brown, James and Belinda Potter, and Nancy and Rick VanOver. They have inspired, encouraged and loved us as we wrote, revised and recycled ideas.

Many thanks to the following friends who have given us their ideas and support:

John Klassen, Kathleen Baxter, Micaela Brakke, Ross Brown, Barb Bureau, Dottie Ecker, Rose DeLiscia Everett, Sheila Feigelson, Norma Godwin, Jerilee Gregory, Melba Hawthorne, Caroline Hill, Lisa Moore, Peg Rice, Bernice Ridout, Shia Shahin, Pat Trombley and Nina Wright.

---

# Dedication

To our beautiful long distance grandchildren:

Benjamin, David, Ethan,
Heather, Laura, Lauren, and Sara.

We love you.

# Table of Contents

**Apricots and Apples** ......................................................10
    To Spoil or not to Spoil

**Books** .........................................................................12
    Gifts Of A Lifetime

**Collections** ................................................................14
    From Soup To Nuts

**Dress-up**......................................................................16
    Let's Pretend

**Ecology**.......................................................................18
    Save A Bug and Other Living Things

**Family Tree**...............................................................20
    Who's Who?

**Grandfathers**.............................................................22
    Teacher, Mentor and Friend

**Holidays**.....................................................................24
    Being There When You Can't Be There

**Intriguing Incidents**.................................................26
    Fact And Fiction

**Jealousy**......................................................................28
    Banish the Green-Eyed Monster

**Kaleidoscope**.............................................................30
    Keeping Up With Change

**Letters**........................................................................32
    The 29¢ Connection

**Manners**......................................................................34
    For Young and Old

**Newsletters**............................................................**36**
    Becoming the Family Publisher

**Oral History**..........................................................**37**
    Straight From the Horse's Mouth

**Photos**....................................................................**38**
    Say "Cheese"

**Quotations**.............................................................**41**
    From the Mouth of Babes

**Rememberences**......................................................**42**
    Little Things Mean a Lot

**Surrogate Grandparenting**....................................**44**
    Fulfilling Your Need to Nurture

**Travel**....................................................................**46**
    The World Through the Eyes of a Child

**Unconditional Love**...............................................**48**
    No Strings Attached

**Visits**....................................................................**49**
    Our House-Their House

**Worry**....................................................................**52**
    Lighten Up

**Extras**....................................................................**53**
    Investing in the Future

**You**........................................................................**55**
    A Unique Role

**Fgotspuz**...............................................................**56**
    The " Perfect " Grandparent

**Additional Readings for Adults**............................**57**

**Children's Books about Grandparents**...................**60**

# Introduction

Being a grandparent is a wonderful experience! Friends, poets and politicians tell us this is so. But how can we be part of this experience if we live far away from our grandchildren?

We know that grandparents are important and that children need all the family support they can get in these challenging times. But how do we create and develop a bond when we only see our grandchildren a few times a year, or less?

The frustration we felt at being long distance grandparents was shared by many of our friends. This prompted us to put together a variety of workable ideas interspersed with some of our own philosophy. Thus, this book was born.

We encourage you to browse through this book, select the ideas that appeal to you and adapt them to fit the ages and interests of your own grandchildren.

We hope these "keep-in-touch" ideas will spark your creativity and bring forth activities that will be unique to your family. Have fun! Enjoy!

# Apricots and Apples

We take great care to make sure that fruits and vegetables don't spoil, but there are some growing things we can "spoil" -- our grandchildren! That's part of the job description for a grandparent! We finally get to do some things that we never, never would have done as parents.

During their visits, we can let our grandchildren stay up with us to see the late show, eat chocolate ice cream in bed, skip the nightly bath (occasionally of course) or wear their favorite pair of blue jeans three days in a row.

Even though we may not wish to be known solely as the "gift" grandparent, we don't have to feel guilty if our first stop in a department store is the children's section. It's OK if we can't resist buying that special frilly dress for an aspiring ballerina or a fancy cowboy hat for the horse lover, even though we just sent off a wonderful birthday gift.

We can listen with understanding and sympathy when our grandchildren are disciplined. We don't undermine the parents but we can say, "We understand how you feel" --(and maybe we can help them understand how their parents feel).

"Spoiling" children has nothing to do with "rotteness" as it does with apricots, apples and most other growing things. It means providing those special warm and loving interactions that our grandchildren will remember and share with their own children. They'll problably not remember that you encouraged them to eat their carrots but they will remember those symbols of love that you shared just with them.

# Books

You can start sending books to your grandchild as soon as you get that telephone call saying "Congratulations, you're a grandparent!" However, knowing which books to select can be confusing.

The bookstores are full of beautiful books for children of all ages-picture books, board books for very young children, story books, poetry books, fairy tales, books about bugs, stars, trucks, numbers and every other imaginable subject. More and more children's books are being written about feelings, friendships, illnesses and other issues that are important to children and their parents. There are even wonderful books about children and their grandparents! (Check our booklist.) Ask fellow grandparents, a librarian, a teacher or the bookstore manager for suggestions.

When you make your selection, remember not only the age and interests of your grandchild but also consider the values you wish to promote. Does the book present minorities and ethnic groups positively? Are girls in the book portrayed as active and competent or do they always take a passive role? Do boys, as well as girls, express feelings? Is violence a prominent feature of the book or do the characters solve problems through talking, negotiating and understanding the other's point of view?

Although you are too far away to snuggle up every night to read a bedtime story to your grandchild, you can do a "second best." Select a book you like. Practice reading it aloud to yourself (or to the cat or dog), then make a cassette tape of the story and mail it along with the book to your grandchild. If the child is old enough to operate the tape recorder and turn the pages of the book, it helps to say at the end of each page "turn the page." You can also use a bell to give the "turn the page" signal. This is a special way to share the wonderful world of books and to let your grandchild know that Grandpa and Grandma recognize the importance of reading.

For those of you who are budding authors try writing your own books. Use photos or your own drawings and make up a simple story about your grandchild.

If your grandchild is just learning to read and you are sending a hand written story, use the same manuscript printing that the child is learning in school. You can often find samples in workbooks sold at supermarkets.

A possible bonus from sending an original book is that your grandchild may make you a book, in return and this unlike many "coffee table" books will get read over and over again.

# Collections

Most children love collecting things!  Look in a child's room and it's likely you'll find a shoebox full of shells, rocks or baseball cards, or a shelf that holds a collection of comic books, dolls or model cars. Collecting not only sparks a child's curiosity about people, places and things but also helps the young collector learn to organize, label, identify and classify.

Starting a collection for your grandchildren - or adding to one they've started will give you an interest in common and certainly makes souvenir buying much easier when you travel.

As an added bonus, today's collections may become valuable financial investments for the future or may lead to a career or a life-long interest or hobby.

Here are a few possibilities for interesting collections.

| | | |
|---|---|---|
| Stamps | Coins | Stones |
| Shells | Leaves & flowers | Cups & saucers |
| Old magazines | Sheet music | Autographs |
| Key rings | Old buttons | Hats |
| T-shirts | Records | Tapes |
| Videos | Political buttons | Watches |
| Clocks | Computer programs | Baseball cards |
| Dolls | Match folders | Post Cards |
| Posters | Theatre programs | Miniatures |

# Dress-up

Little children, especially those 2-6 years old, love to play "dress-up" and particularly love clothes that belong to mommy and daddy, or grandma and grandpa. Dressing-up is part of "pretending" to be someone else; a dad or mom, a fireman, a ballet dancer, a pilot. Children like to imitate adults working or playing. This is a step towards recognizing the roles other people play in their world. It also encourages the development of imagination, language and social skills.

Pack a box with old hats, scarves, cowboy boots, high-heeled shoes, a vest, a shawl, wigs, a brief case or anything else that you think a child could use for "pretend" play. Don't forget items such as old jewelry, purses, flash lights and camping or back-packing equipment. You may be lucky enough to have stowed away items from your travels such as a handwoven poncho, a colorful kimono or a French beret. Perhaps, it's time to part with these treasures so your grandchildren, through their play, can experience another world.

Some great finds can be purchased at resale shops, rummage sales and garage sales. Washing these item before sending them is advisable. There are also commercial "dress-up" boxes you can buy, but your second handers are usually more fun and are certainly cheaper!

# Ecology
<u>**Save A Bug and Other Living Things**</u>

Our grandchildren need to see us making a statement about the close relationship between the environment and all living things.  We can show that we believe in conserving our resources and that we practice what we believe by doing some very simple things.

---

- Purchase toys with the minimal packaging needed to keep them from being broken.

- Be creative as you wrap packages by using wallpaper scraps, paper bags and newspapers.  The comics make great wrapping paper.

- Give your grandchild a seedling that you can plant when you are together and the child can watch it grow. If you plant a young tree when your grandchild visits, then you can send photos to show the miracle of growth. This can be a great memory builder.

- Buy the Book, <u>50 Simple Things Kids Can do to Protect the Earth</u> by the Earth Works Group and encourage your adult children to try some of these ideas with their children.

- Set a good example by recycling your own newspapers, glass containers, plastics and cans.

And most important, show respect and reverence for all living things especially when you're with your grandchild. If a bug gets into your house try letting it outdoors instead of squashing it. Be brave! A friend who is scared to death of spiders said "that's easy for you to say!"

The attitudes and behaviors you exhibit will have lasting benefits for your grandchildren and all other inhabitants of our planet.

# Family Tree

A "picture family tree" is fun to make when a child begins to ask questions about the relationship between parents and grandparents.

The family tree can be expanded to include cousins and aunts and uncles as the children become older and more interested in family relationships. You can help your grandchildren appreciate their heritage by putting the geneology on cassette tape or video tape. The use of photos and funny stories about each person shown on the tree brings them to life.

As R. Daniel Cuvazos, Editor of the <u>McAllen Texas Monitor</u> says, "Learning about history through books is wonderful, but learning it from a grandparent who has made a personal investment in your life, is even better."

As you work on this project, you may become so fascinated that you'll want to delve deeper into your roots. Check with your librarian or local geneological society for information on how to proceed.

# Grandfathers
## Teacher, Mentor and Friend

*We realize that all parts of this book apply to both grandmothers and grandfathers, but we decided to give grandpas a page all their own.*

Grandfathers, you are truly important role models and teachers especially when there isn't a father in the home. You become a strong influence through your actions and attitudes and by sharing your talents and interests whether they are music, photography, reading, auto mechanics, golfing or simply walking and appreciating the outdoors. You can share these interests when you are with your grandchild and also through your letters, phone calls or videos. If you're a carpenter try making a home video about building a birdhouse. You might send all the materials needed for the project along with the video. You can't hammer a nail straight? Then try demonstrating golf swings, magic tricks or the "failure proof" way to make a souffle. The possibilities are endless!

Establish some routines and traditions that the children will look forward to when you're together such as a bike ride, a trip to the ice cream store or an after dinner game of checkers or chess. It's also important to establish some routines or traditions that you can carry on when you're apart such as starting your phone calls with a "knock-knock" joke or including a sports article or crossword puzzle in each letter. Of course, these added attractions will vary as the interests of both you and your grandchild change. Ten years of "Knock-Knock" jokes might be a little too much!

In addition to sharing "let's do" or "how to" interests, remember that even more important are the attitudes that a grandfather demonstrates. A grandfather can show that men are good nurturers of children, that problems can be solved peacefully, that being kind and affectionate is not "sissy" and that people are to be valued on their own merits and not judged by their race, religion, place of birth or economic status.

What do you get in return? You get to hear a child say, "I love you, Grandpa" and you get a chance to play a role in the growth of a precious & unique human being. What a wonderful opportunity to become part of the future!

# Holidays
## Being There When You Can't Be There

Most of us would love to be with our grandchildren for the holidays, but sometimes it's impossible, so we need to find ways to be there in spirit. Now is the time for your creativity to come forth so you can be at the celebration in spirit if not in person.

Valentine's Day is a perfect time to send a message of love to your grandchildren. Buy 3 or 4 valentines and send them, one at a time, far enough ahead of February 14 so each child can enjoy the cards before the rest of the world heads for the post office.

For Halloween, consider sending a costume for a little witch or bunny. Check with the parents first. The children probably don't need more candy but a paper pumpkin or ghost will let them know you are enjoying the season. A battery operated ghost that made spooky noises when you clapped your hands turned out to be the Halloween "gift of the year" for one grandchild. For a really creative touch, try making a scary or funny greeting card using your own picture or the child's picture. It's pretty funny seeing a witch's hat on Grandma's head or Grandpa in a clown suit. You might even start a whole new fashion trend!

Thanksgiving can be a time when we let our grandchildren know that we are thankful for them. You might want to send a card expressing your feelings about being lucky enough to be their grandparents and telling them how much you appreciate their thoughtfulness, kindness or sense of humor.

Holiday ornaments, placemats or place cards are fine gifts and can be purchased or handmade. A special ornament sent each year can become part of an on-going collection that will be treasured. If you celebrate Christmas, an advent calendar sent every year can be an anticipated tradition.

If you have a reputation for baking special Christmas or Chanukah cookies or fruit cake, pack a box with these treats and send them along. One grandparent sends delicious almond bark candy made from almonds grown in her back yard. Everyone in the family looks forward to this.

For most children, the best holiday is their own birthday! Instead of sending the traditional card and gift, you might like to do something as unusual as arranging to have a clown deliver a bunch of helium balloons to the birthday child, or enlist help from your son or daughter to hide your birthday notes around the house. As a surprise, at the end of the search the child finds the package that you have sent. This gives the feeling you are there and is a great way to send a birthday gift. You might even have a birthday cake delivered! (Again, check with the parents first).

Of course, one of the easiest and best ways to be there is to make a phone call to wish your grandchild a happy holiday. In the not too distant future, we may all have video phones to give that added sense of bonding. However, if you haven't bought a new bathrobe in 20 years you may find this prospect a little frightening!

# Intriguing Incidents

**Fact And Fiction**

From miles away you can give your grandchild an extra special experience to enjoy.  Here are a few ideas for creating "intriguing incidents."

Write a factual story with a bit of fantasy thrown in, about your cat or dog or any other animal.  A story one granddaughter liked was about a gigantic spider that became a household pet.  She always asked about that spider so of course got added installments.  Another grandmother wrote about a mischievous magpie who stole her wire rimmed glasses and hid them in the petunia box.

Write about your interests or adventures in story form with a bit of humor thrown in.  You might draw on experiences such as going camping, picking strawberries, rafting down the Mississippi River, planting your garden or even cleaning house.  Your grandchildren will treasure stories about grandma and grandpa, especially if something funny happened to them.  Falling off a raft may not have been funny to you at the time but you can turn this incident into a humorous adventure.  Maybe you surfaced with fish in your pockets!  Let your imagination run wild.  Realism has no place in these tales.

Write a story about a difficult problem you faced as you were growing up -- being the shortest or tallest in your class, wearing glasses when no one else had to, or always being the last to be chosen for a team because you couldn't catch the ball. You might tell about the time you played hookey from school or the time you wrestled with your brother and broke his thumb. Write about your feelings and how you dealt with the problems. These stories can help your grandchildren relate to you and other adults and may also help them work out similar problems.

---

Try writing a story with your grandchild as the central character. Children love to see their name in print. The story might be about a real adventure or one you make up about an event or activity in which your grandchild can star. You might write about your grandchild going to a circus, a ball game, a birthday party. She could be the main character in a story about a trip to outer space, a piano debut at Carnegie Hall or an invention of a magical multiplication hat! Use the interests of your granchildren as you search for story ideas.

# Jealousy

## Banish the Green-Eyed Monster

We like to think that because we're "40 plus," the 8 letter word, J-e-a-l-o-u-s-y will never enter our lives, but think again!

We may live across the country from our grandchildren and get to see them only once or twice a year while the other grandparents live down the street and can drop in every day, spend holidays together and share the day to day happenings - or - we may be on a tight budget while the other grandparents can afford to buy elaborate presents or take everyone on wonderful vacations. We may feel left out, inadequate and yes, jealous!

What to do about this uncomfortable feeling? First, admit this feeling is real! Each of us experiences a variety of emotions that make our lives rich, satisfying and sometimes uncomfortable. Next, look positively at the pluses for your grandchildren if they have grandparents who live close by.

We all want the best for our families but there are things we can't do when we live far away. How fortunate it is that the near-by grandparents can supply support by taking the young ones to lessons, picking them up from day care or baby-sitting either on a regular basis or when an emergency arises. The proximity of the other grandparents and their willingness to help takes a load off our minds. We know our children and grandchildren are in good hands! After all, no child can receive too much love and support.

As we work through these twinges of jealousy we can appreciate the uniqueness of each grandparent and the richness we each add to the lives of the children we mutually love. Our challenge is to be creative and positive in our efforts to keep a relationship with our grandchildren vibrant through the mail, by phone and in a variety of other ways that are right for us.

# Kaleidoscope
## Keeping Up With Change

The dictionary gives one definition of this word as a "series of changing events or places." We're going to stretch this definition to include "a series of changing growth patterns and interests."

If we see our grandchildren only once or twice a year, we have a challenging job keeping abreast of changes in their interests, their sizes and the things that are important to them and their friends.

You've probably all heard stories similar to the one about the 16 year old girl getting a "Barbie doll" for her birthday. Her granddad couldn't understand why she didn't sound more excited when she called to thank him. Also, remember that although a child started collecting baseball cards when he was eight, this doesn't necessarily mean he will still be interested in collecting them when he's 18.

It's hard to keep up with all the changes when you're far away, but taking time to find out what your grandchildren like to do after school, what their favorite TV programs are and the names of their friends gives you something to talk about on the phone and write about in letters. This information comes in handy when you shop for gifts, but most of all, it lets your grandchildren know that you care enough to keep up with new interests in their lives.

How do you do this? One way is to become a good telephone sleuth. Think of the questions you'd like to ask before you get on the phone. Try asking questions that require more than a "yes" or "no" answer. For example: "tell me about your trip to the zoo". If your grandchildren are older you might subscribe to the local Sunday paper so you can keep up with what is happening in their city. Of course, your grandchildren's parents are a major source of information.

# Letters

Children enjoy receiving mail so sending letters is an easy way for you to express your love and show that you are thinking of them. You can send traditional letters or you can personalize your letters in a variety of ways.

For the young child, make a letter with the nouns represented by pictures so the child can help read it. For example, draw or find a picture for cat, tree, grandpa, grandma, instead of writing the word, e.g. The ⟨cat⟩ ran up the ⟨tree⟩

Include a sheet of stickers with your letter. It's a comparatively inexpensive way to add a special surprise, especially when you have a number of grandchildren. Older children love receiving a coupon for a hamburger or milk shake from their favorite fast food restaurant. For variety, send a dot to dot picture, a riddle, a cross word puzzle or a brain teaser. For added fun and suspense, send the answer a day or two later.

If you like to write poetry, create a poem about the fun things you did together on your last visit. This will help keep memories alive. If your poem rhymes, you can leave out the rhyming words for the child to insert. You can hide the key words inside the envelope or on the back of the letter. e.g. We took a walk upon the beach and then we ate a juicy_____. The water was cold but the sun was hot. I really love the beach a _____. Beginning readers really enjoy these poetic puzzles.

# Other ideas for pepping up your letters are:

- Put a little dab of your favorite perfume on your letter and envelope. This familiar smell helps bring you close.-- Photos from the last visit are always special to receive. It's good to have Grandpa and Grandma in the picture, too.

- Send along a cartoon or newspaper article or photo you think your grandchild will like.

- Include a pressed flower from your garden or flower pot.

- For a special surprise send along a tracing of your hand. Ask your grandchild to place his hand on yours, trace it and send it back to you. You might also include Fido's paw print.

- Try a letter with some open-ended sentences to be filled out and returned such as:

> When I'm bigger_____.
> On Saturday I like to _____.
> This summer I'm going to_____.
> My favorite book is _____.
> If I could be an animal, I would be a _____.

To encourage getting a response, include a self-addressed, stamped envelope.

- For the older child, try writing a letter in code. e.g.
9_____12-15-22-5_____25-15-21  (You'll probably think of a more complex code. This is a simple 1 = A, 2 = B, etc.)

- For a statement about the 90's you might forego the postal system once in a while and FAX a message to your grandchild.

All these ideas take more time than money. The plain old fashioned newsy letter is still very much in style, especially when it ends with "I love you."

# Manners

Few of us expect our granchildren to bow or curtsy, to follow the old adage of "don't speak until you're spoken to" or to sit still during a formal dinner party.  But many of us find it difficult to deal with the openness and what seems like "talking back" that is characteristic of today's children.  To many of us, this seems like a lack of manners.

But let's be aware that child-rearing practices have changed since our days as parents.  Children of this generation are encouraged to vent their feelings and to say what they think.  We must also remember that we are the grandparents, not the parents and in the presence of the parents it is not our responsibility to discipline, correct or lecture.  However, there may be occasions when we really feel we are being treated rudely.  What can we do?  We can let our grandchildren know that this treatment is unacceptable and that we love them too much to let this continue.  We may have to say "no", or "stop" in a tone that is both firm and respectful.

What else can we do to support our adult children in their efforts to help their children become sensitive to other people's feelings and points of view?

We can help by saying "thank you" and "please" to our grandchildren, their friends, parents and all others who inhabit their world.

- Writing thank-you notes to the children after we've

visited them or received a gift.

- Asking for and giving real consideration to their opinions and suggestions.

- Looking for the real meaning behind the child's words and helping him to express this, e.g. "I hate you" usually doesn't mean that at all. It may mean "I'm mad because you wouldn't let me walk in the mud puddles."

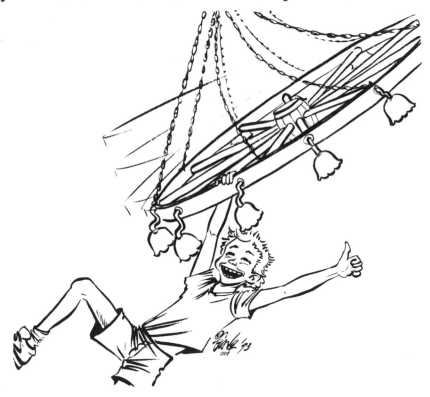

We can also acquaint ourselves with the stages of child growth and development so that we know what behaviors we can expect at different ages. There are many books in the libraries and book stores that give this information. (See our list of additional readings.)

# Newsletter

## Becoming the Family Publisher

A grandmother in our neighborhood has become the publisher, editor and artist for a family newsletter that is mailed to all family members four times a year.

She gets news of her family by asking relatives to send information to her by a definate date. News can include information about new babies, new jobs, special events such as recitals or sports activities, riddles, jokes, recipes and anything else that would be of interest. Phone calls sometimes have to be made to remind family members to send in their stories. Then grandma or grandpa types up the articles, adds a few line drawings or photos and make copies of the newsletter to send to the grandchildren, aunts, uncles, cousins and close family friends.

One article could be an invitaiton to help plan a family reunion so your grandchildren get to see in real living color all those "unforgettable characters" they've heard so much about.

These newsletters are received with much excitement and help give a family, often spread all over the world, a sense of belonging. If the newsletters are saved, they make a great written history of family life for the grandchildren to enjoy when they are grown.

# Oral History
## Straight From the Horse's Mouth

You are one of a kind, a living history whose accomplishments, joys and disappointments will both interest and perhaps astound your grandchildren. The easiest way to make a record of your life and the times in which you've lived is to use a tape recorder. Talk about both happy and not-so-happy times. Don't worry too much about organization. Just begin!

What kinds of things can you talk about? For starters, include stories about your childhood, schooling, jobs, games you loved to play and stories about those unforgettable ancestors who make your past colorful. Every family has interesting stories that make up their history such as the one about Great-Great Grandfather Dan, driving his cattle on foot from Michigan to Missouri to take 1st place at the World's Fair or Uncle Tony who helped build the tunnel under the Detroit River.

You may enjoy singing your favorite songs, playing an instrument, reading a poem or sharing a joke or riddle. You can include news about world and historical or scientific events that happened during your lifetime. You may also want to record a special message to each grandchild. These tapes can become as precious to your grandchildren as those family photo albums that are passed along from generation to generation.

------

*"You are alive as long as you live in someone's memory. Don't procrastinate."*    *Anonymous*

# Photos

Pictures really do say more than a thousand words. Try making a "This is my Life" album for your grandchild. Include pictures of your house, garden or pet. Have a friend take pictures of you reading, biking, playing tennis or doing whatever you do that makes you come to life for a child living 200 or 2,000 plus miles away. For "career awareness" include some pictures of you on the job or doing volunteer work. Dress up the photos with a sentence or two about each picture.

Or - make an album about your grandchild's mother or father. Children love to see pictures of their parents when they were little. "This is Daddy when he first learned to ride his bike!"

Another album idea is to collect pictures of your grandchild as he/she grew up and label them - "This is you chasing the duck at Grandma's house," or "This is you helping light the Chanukkah candles."

Picture post cards of your travels, picture cards from museums, pictures from newspapers and magazines, old greeting cards or calendars are all photo possibilities for sharing interests with that special child.

During your visits with your family, be sure to take some pictures that show you and your grandchildren together so as they look at the photos they can relive those special times. You can use these pictures in several ways: label and put them into an album, use them on homemade greeting cards or ornaments, or make them into refrigerator decorations by gluing the pictures onto the inside of jar lids and attaching a magnet or magnetic tape to the back.

A camera and several rolls of film make a great gift for a child. Hopefully, you'll start receiving as well as sending pictures.

# Ashley

*Ashley wanted to wear her new black patent leather shoes to nursery school. Her mother said - "no, these are just for good". Ashley quickly responded, "I am good Mommy" what more could her mom say but "Yes".*

# Jessica

*Jessica was being tested to enter Kindergarten and was asked, "What does your Father do?" "He's a computer manager" said Jessica. "What does your mother do?" "She is Promotional Manager for the Renaissance Center." answered Jessica who quickly asked "Do you want to know what my Grandpa and Grandma do?          ...They go to church."*

# Anthony

*Anthony was about 3 1/2. He wanted to use the expression "It's better than nothing". What came out was, "It's as good as nothing".*

# Bob

*Two year old Bob was playing with a little friend John who bit his finger real hard. Through his tears he told his mother "John eat Me!"*

# Quotations
## From the Mouths of Babes

How often have you said, "I wish I had written down all the clever and funny things my children said when they were little!"?  As parents, it's difficult to keep up with all the day to day responsibilities of changing diapers, baking cupcakes for the class picnic, putting in a full day at the office or factory and working to help pass the school millage.  Writing down the cute sayings of a child does not often rank as a high priority.

But, as grandparents, we have a second chance to make a record for posterity by keeping a "quotations" book.  You can buy a lovely blank book at a stationery store, or you can use a spiral notebook or your word processor.  When you talk to your grandchildren and they say something funny or when the parents tell you, "You'll never believe what Johnnie said this morning," write it down and include the date.  One grandparent recorded her grandchilds use of the words "carter seat" for "car seat" and "rub back" for guess what?  Who knows, these expressions may one day be part of our American vocabulary.  Another grandparent wrote down the comments of her granddaughter who took her first airplane ride at age two.  The ride went smoothly until the plane hit a  big air pocket.  The adults turned pale but smiles returned when they heard the child pipe up with "Let's do it again!"

Preserve these bits of innocence and wisdom and you'll have a wonderful family record to pass along to your grandchildren.

41

# Remembrances
## Little Things Mean a Lot

One way to keep memories alive and strengthen the connection between the past and the future is to pass along some special remembrances to our grandchildren. These are often more important to them than big or expensive gifts.

One granddaughter was interested in cooking. When her grandmother sent a recipe file with family favorites she was delighted. As new favorites surfaced they were added to the gift file. The file included such culinary masterpieces as Uncle George's super, colossal popcorn balls, Grandpa's wedding soup and Cousin Sue's mile high mystery cake.

As children get older you may decide to give them treasures such as a petrified stone that was found by Great Uncle Dave on his trip to California in 1930 or something as special as a wristwatch that belonged to your grandmother. You may wish to let them choose between two or three items. Write the story behind the memento and enclose it with the gift so that the significance of the remembrance does not get lost.

A word of caution about giving something you place great value on- others may or may not place the same value on the item as you do, so be sure you really want to part with the memento. Then give it with love and no strings attached realizing it may get broken or lost or tossed in a drawer with a heap of other "treasures" such as string, baseball cards and gum wrappers.

# Surrogate Grandparenting
## Fulfilling Your Need to Nurture

One way we can alleviate some of the loneliness of being separated by distance from our grandchildren is to become a "surrogate" or substitute grandparent for a child who has no grandparents living close by. What a gift for both of you! You have an opportunity to become closely involved in the life of a young child and the child benefits by having another significant adult in his life who is willing to share talents, experiences, resources, support and love.

You may already be serving in this role with a neighbor or friend's child. But if you like the idea of surrogate grandparenting and don't have a child in mind, try contacting a nearby school, child care center, church, hospital, juvenile home or neighborhood center, asking whether the institution can use your services and telling them how much time and energy you're willing to spend. Don't be afraid to tell about any special talents or skills you have. You may be asked to read stories, tutor a child in math, listen to a child read or be the group hugger and smile giver.

Big Brother and Big Sister programs have operated successfully for years. A "Grandmother, Grandfather" program can be just as successful. You might be interested in getting a group of older adults together and working with a school to organize a placement program for them. A program already in existence in some areas is the Foster Grandparent Program, coordinated through ACTION, a nationwide domestic volunteer program.

A fairly new program operating in the Ann Arbor, Michigan area is the "Latch, Match" program in which a homebound grandparent (or other senior) is matched with an elementary school age child who must stay alone after school until the parents come home from work. The older person calls the child every day after school to make sure the child is OK and to chat about the day's events. For more information about this program call the University of Michigan, Geriatric Clinic, 313-761-2556.

The possibilities are endless for involvement in a project that reduces isolation for both the young and the not-so-young! We are all responsible for helping children, biological or "adopted", grow up supported by adults who care about them. Let's meet this challenge!

# Travel
## The World Through the Eyes of a Child

A great way to get to know your grandchildren and to build wonderful memories is to travel. If possible, take one child at a time which means no bickering for you to deal with and undivided attention for the special child. But, make sure the child wants to go! A reluctant child on a trip is not a happy camper.

Some grandparents begin these joint travel ventures with camping trips to nearby parks. As the child grows older, the camping trips become longer and more elaborate. Grandparents have an opportunity to show their grandchildren the beauty in this country -- perhaps the Grand Canyon, the deserts of the American Southwest, the beautiful California coastal drive. Camping experiences are perfect for modeling cooperation and teamwork as everyone pitches in to cook dinner, break camp and read maps. You'll build lasting memories and provide your grandchild with exciting things to share when the teacher says "Write a story about your summer vacation."

For non-campers, traveling can be as simple as a day-trip by car or train to the next town, or as elaborate as a week at a texas Ranch or a trip to Europe. Accommodations can be as basic as a room at a Youth Hostel or as fancy as lodgings at an elegant hotel. Some boat cruises and resort hotels offer planned activities and reduced rates for people traveling with children.

The following travel companies design wonderful

trips for grandchildren and grandparents:
- Grand Travel, domestic and overseas trips 1-800-247-7651.
- Vistatours, South Dakota and New England, 1-800-248-4782;
- Rascals in Paradise, South Pacific, Europe, 1-800-U-Rascal.

For more information contact your travel agency or bookstore for information about trips tailored to meet the needs of both grandchildren and grandparents. A magazine that may be helpful is <u>Mature Traveler</u>, P. O. Box 50820, Reno, NV, 89512.

A word of caution. If you are traveling out of state or out of the country, be sure to carry with you a notarized letter signed by both parents (or the custodial parent) giving you permission to travel with the child and authorizing you to seek emergency medical treatment.

No matter how simple or elaborate your travel plans are, you have a unique opportunity to experience the many natural and man-made wonders in our world with an eager, enthusiastic traveling companion.

# Unconditional Love
## No Strings Attached

Grandparents are best known for giving "unconditional love."  This is something money can't buy.  It is expressed through your voice, your smiles and your attitudes of acceptance and respect when you and your grandchild are together, when you talk on the phone and through your letters.

Unconditional love means you love your grandchildren no matter what.  They don't have to earn your love.  It's there, even during the times when they act in ways that seem strange or troublesome. Unconditional love means that when appropriate, we try to help our young people work out solutions to their problems and that we love them even if they choose not to follow our suggestions or to do what we feel is "correct."  It is important to remember that our grandchildren are growing up in a world that is very different from the one in which we grew up.

Let them know that you believe they will grow up to be healthy, responsible and caring adults.  Let criticism and negativity make way for unconditional love, the most precious gift we can give.

# Visits

We all know that regardless of how many letters we write or phone calls we make, real live visits are the stuff of which memories are made and bonds created. How do we make the most of these visits? Here are a few suggestions.

## Our House

A little advance preparation can make the visit more fun for everyone -- but a note of caution -- too much preparation can be so exhausting we can't enjoy our visitors. (Remember the dinner party when the house was spotless the food was perfect, but the hostess fell asleep before dessert was served!) We really don't have to remove every speck of dust or cook all our family's favorite foods. A swipe of the dust cloth and a pot of chili might do!

- When young children visit it's of #1 importance to put away anything that might be harmful to a child. Vitamins, mouthwash, perfumes and after shave lotions can be just as dangerous as medicines and cleaning supplies.

- If order is important to you, it's OK to say "We'll have dinner after we pick up the toys and clothes." Make this a game. "Let's see if we can put everything away by the time we count to 10" -- or -- use an egg timer to give the signal.

- Provide a drawer, a box or a basket as a treasure chest for your grandchild. Games, pictures, books, buttons, a little doll or truck -- anything you think will appeal can be kept in this special place. A small present wrapped and marked with the child's name adds to the anticipation of looking through "Grandma's drawer."

- Create a routine or ritual that can repeat with your grandchildren each time they visit. One grandmother has a special lunch date with her granddaughter at their favorite restaurant. A grandson and his grandfather look forward to their traditional checkers game each time they're together.

- When your grandchild is old enough to visit you alone, you'll have a wonderful chance to get to know and bond with this special child. Plan the time so that you have specific ideas for things to do. Keep in mind of course, the interest and desires of the child. Advance planning will save you the frustration of dealing with last minute indecision. Plans can be as simple as baking a cake, walking to the playground, having a picnic in the park or as sophisticated as attending a concert or visiting an art gallery. However, be flexible! Rain, fatigue or a special request from your grandchild may tell you to put your plans on hold. Just "Hanging out" at home may be a top priority.

## Their House

Ask your grandchildren what they would like to do with you during your visit. They may request walking to the playground or reading together at bedtime. If the request is as exotic as "let's ride on an elephant," you'll have an opportunity to provide a creative alternative. Try to spend some time alone with each grandchild!

- Tuck in your suitcase a "do-it-together" project such as a package of flower seeds, a model plane kit, puppet materials, a new game or anything else you think will encourage involvement between you and your grandchildren.

- Respect your adult children's rules about your grandchildren's bedtime, eating habits, clothes selections, etc. Again, remember, you are the grandparents, not the parents!

- Be a model guest! Offer to help prepare meals, straighten up, take the family out to dinner, etc. but be careful not to "take over" and never criticize, no matter how great the temptation.

- If you're tired and need quiet time, it's OK to say, "Grandpa needs to rest for a while" - or "I'm going to take a little walk by myself. When I get back we'll work on the puzzle."

- Follow the golden rule of visiting. Leave before your family is tired of company. No matter how well you get along, company for too long a time can be stressful for everyone.

Whether the visits are at "your" house or "their" house, relax, have fun and don't expect perfection of yourself or any other family member.

# Worry

Some people tell us "The best part of having grandchildren is that you enjoy them but you don't worry about them!"

Right? Wrong! For people like us who are natural worriers--we can now worry twice as much. Added to our general worries about unemployment, famine, earthquakes and the national debt, we now worry about personal issues such as cloth vs. paper diapers, breast vs. bottle feeding, too early or too late bedtimes, competent or flaky babysitters, and ad infinitum.

Many of us stay awake nights trying to figure out solutions to patch up or change someone else's life, but deep down, we all know that we can't help a situation with our worry. All we do is make ourselves sick and everyone around us miserable.

If you are looking for ways to stop being a natural, 24 hour a day worrier, try this: make a list of your worries and give yourself 10 minutes a day to worry. Then, release those things you can't do anything about and go into action to do the things you can.

There is an advantage to being a long-distance worrier. You see less and hear less than your "next-door" counterpart, so you have less to worry about. This is one time you can say, "Hooray for being far away!"

# Extras

Young families are usually struggling to pay basic living expenses. The United States Department of Agriculture statistics say that the cost of rearing a child born in 1991 will come close to $300,000 and this does not include college costs. Many grandparents are now in a better financial position than

are their adult children. If you fit this picture, you may wish to help provide some of the X-tras in your families' lives. Sometimes this financial help may be in the form of a loan, sometimes it may be an outright gift. Make sure the status of the financial assistance is clearly understood.

Some grandparents choose to help with one or more of the following: fees for day care, summer camp, special classes in art or science, tutors when a child needs additional help with school work, clothing, dental braces or anything else that may not fit into a young family's budget.

College is, of course, the ultimate "x-tra" and you may be able to provide some financial help with this costly item. Stocks or Series EE Savings Bonds make wonderful birthday and holiday gifts and if purchased on a regular basis can make up a substantial portion of a college fund. You may wish to investigate the Uniform Gifts to Minors Act, or the establishment of a college trust fund. We recommend that you talk to a financial advisor for advice regarding your own situation. If you are not in a position to give financial support, you can still help by giving encouragement that builds the self-esteem that makes going to college or pursuing further study in a suitable field a strong possibility.

Another very special X-tra to provide is a treat for the parents. Parents often find it difficult or impossible to get away for some private time to themselves. You may wish to send them an "unbirthday" gift of a check to cover the cost of dinner, theatre tickets and babysitter; or perhaps money for golf, a massage or a visit to the beauty salon! Some grandparents "insist" the parents go off by themselves for a few days so they can have the grandchildren all to themselves. Sneaky, eh? This is a bonus for all generations.

A less costly but wonderful idea is to send a note or card telling your adult children what good parents they are and how proud you are of them. They may fall over from shock but you can be sure they'll feel very special and appreciated.

# You

You, as grandparents, are in a position of great importance. As soon as that baby is born, you become a unique role model for that child. You don't have to apply for the job --it becomes yours as soon as that baby draws its first breath. Whether you are involved in your own career or choose to be a stay-at-home grandparent, whether you live down the street or on the other side of the world, your grandchildren will look to you as an example of a trustworthy family member who is loving and nurturing. You will share their interests and bring to their lives, excitement about learning, a sense of humor, a strong sense of values and an enthusiasm for life.

How can you act as a positive role model when you live far away? It is difficult, but it is possible! You let these young people into your life through your letters and stories, the video tapes, the pictures you send and your phone calls. You help out if you can, in times of emergency such as illness or divorce and you try to arrange your vacations so that some of your time can be spent with your grandchildren.

A close relationship with you will help your grandchildren form positive attitudes toward other older people and toward their own lives. They can look forward to growing up and doing for their children and grandchildren what you are doing for them--providing a solid connection between generations.

And what do we get in return? A chance to let the child in us laugh, tell silly jokes, play on the swings and love and be loved.

# Fgotspfuz

## The "Perfect" Grandparent

This word, according to the yet unwritten, unpublished <u>Grandparents Dictionary</u> means - "a species of super-colossal grandparents who bake and send cookies weekly, write a story a day, send tapes on every special occasion, always have a camera ready for snapping meaningful pictures, buy only the perfect gifts and are always patient, never critical or judgmental!"

In truth, we have never met such a creature in our travels but we have met hundreds of grandparents like you, who in addition to leading active lives, have made a commitment to strengthening the bond between generations, no matter how great the distance.

We celebrate you!

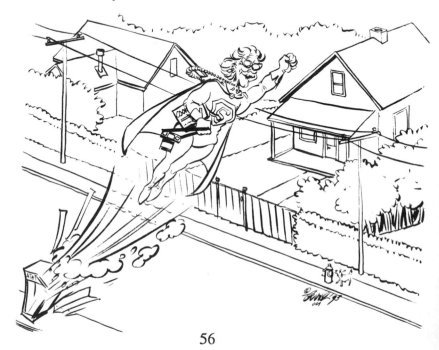

# Additional Reading for Adults

The following is a list of books which offer additional information about some of the areas touched on in this book.

BECOMING A BETTER GRANDPARENT: A GUIDEBOOK FOR STRENGTHENING THE FAMILY. Robert Strom and Shirley Strom. Sage Publications, Inc. 1991.

BEST OF THE BEST FOR CHILDREN: LIBRARIANS RECOMMEND BOOKS, MAGAZINES, VIDEO, AUDIO, SOFTWARE, TOYS, TRAVEL. Denise Perry Donavin, editor. Random House. NewYork. 1992

BETWEEN PARENTS AND GRANDPARENTS. Arthur Kornhaber, M.D. Berkeley Publishing Group. 1986.

BLACK HEROES AND HEROINES. (Books 1-6). Ida Bellegarde. Bell Enterprises. 1979-1985.

DOING CHILDREN'S MUSEUMS. A GUIDE TO 225 HANDS-ON MUSEUMS. Joanee Cleave. Williamson Publishing. 1988.

FREE TO BE--YOU AND ME. 27 authors, composers and illustrators, conceived by Marlo Thomas. Bantam Edition. 1987.

FUNNY YOU DON'T LOOK LIKE A GRANDMOTHER. Lois Wyse. Crown Publishers. 1988.

GRANDCHILDREN ARE SO MUCH FUN, I SHOULD HAVE HAD THEM FIRST. Lois Wyse. Crown Publishers. 1992.

GRANDFATHERS. Anne Joselp. Zebra. 1991.

GRANDFATHER REMEMBERS: MEMORIES FOR MY GRANDCHILD. Judith Levy. Harper Collins. 1986.

GRANDPARENTING. David Elkind. Scott, Foresman. 1990.

GRANDPARENTING FOR THE 90'S--PARENTING IS FOREVER. Robert Aldrich, M.D. and Glenn Austin, M.D. Robert Erdman Publishing. 1991.

GRANDPARENTING: UNDERSTANDING TODAY'S CHILDREN. David Elkind. Scott Foresman and Co. 1989.

HOW TO GRANDPARENT. Fitzhugh Dodson with Paula Reuben. Signet Books. 1984.

HOW TO TALK SO KIDS WILL LISTEN AND LISTEN SO KIDS WILL TALK. Adele Faber and Elaine Mazzlish. Avon Books. 1982.

HOW TO TAPE INSTANT ORAL BIOGRAPHIES. William Zimmerman. Gaurionex Press. 1982.

IT'S YOUR STORY, PASS IT ON. Mary L. Colgin and Thea S. Vander Ven. Colgin Publishing. 1986.

JUST ENOUGH TO MAKE A STORY: A SOURCEBOOK FOR STORYTELLING. Nany Schimmel. Sisters Choice. 1987.

KID HEROES OF THE ENVIRONMENT. Earth Works Group. 1992.

LEARNING AND LOVING TO READ. Jill F. Hauser. Learning Excell. 1990.

NEW READ ALOUD HANDBOOK. Jim Trelese. Viking Penquin Books. 1989.

PARENT'S GUIDE TO WILLS AND TRUSTS - FOR GRANDPARENTS TOO. Don Silver. Adams - Hall Publishing. 1992.

RAINY DAY ACTIVITIES FOR PRESCHOOLERS. Compiled and Edited A.M. Co Ann Marie Connolly and Helen Gibson. Mercer Island Preschool Association. 1988.

SIMPLE SCIENCE EXPERIMENTS WITH EVERYDAY MATERIALS. Muriel Mandell. Sterling Publishing. 1989.

TO OUR CHILDREN'S CHILDREN: PRESERVING FAMILY HISTORIES FOR GENERATIONS TO COME. Bob Greene and D.G. Fulford. Doubleday. 1993.

TOUCHPOINTS, YOUR CHILD'S EMOTIONAL AND BEHAVIORAL DEVELOPMENT. T. Berry Brazelton, M.D. Addison Wesley Publishers. 1992

TRAVELING WITH CHILDREN AND ENJOYING IT: A COMPLETE GUIDE TO FAMILY TRAVEL BY CAR, PLANE AND TRAIN. Arlene Kay Butler. Globe Pequot Press. 1991.

101 WAYS TO MAKE YOUR CHILD FEEL SPECIAL. Vicki Lansky. Contemporary Books, Inc. 1991.

WHAT DO YOU REALLY WANT FOR YOUR CHILDREN? Dr. Wayne W. Dyer. 1986. Avon Books.

YOU AND YOUR GRANDCHILDREN. Sunie Levin. Price Stern Sloan, Inc. 1991.


## BOOK BUYING SERVICES

Some specialty catalogues offer personalized recommendations. One convenient source is the Children's Small Press Collection. 1-800-221-8056

# Children's Books About Grandparents

ABUELA. Arthur Dorros. Dalton's Children's Books, 1991
  A young girl and her Grandmother, her "abuela," take a wonderful imaginary trip over New York City. The narrative includes Spanish phrases.

COAL MINE PEACHES. Michelle Dionetti. Orchard Books Watts. 1991
  This is the story of three generations of an Italian family. A young girl describes her grandfather's arrival in the United States and the stories he told about his life in this country.

GRANDMA'S BILL. Martin Waddell. Orchard Books Watts. 1990
  Grandma shows little Bill her photo album with pictures of his grandfather also named Bill.

GRANDPA'S FACE. Eloise Greenfield. Philomel Books. 1988
  A granddaughter learns that despite her actor grandfather's mean stage role, his love for her is something that will never change.

GRANDPA'S SONG. Tony Johnston. Dial Bnooks for Young Readers. 1991
  The young child helps her grandpa when he forgets the words to his favorite song. A lovely story about support between the young and the old.

GRAN - GRAN'S BEST TRICK. L.Dwight Holden. Magination Press. 1989.
  A child tells about her special relationship with her grandfather who dies from cancer and how hard it was for her to cope with his death.

MY GRANDMA HAS BLACK HAIR. Mary Hoffman and

Joanna Burroughs. Beaver Books. 1988.
This is a wonderful book about a little girl whose granny is not at all like the grannies in many books. She doesn't bake or sew but she tells "smashing" stories about life in the circus and of course she has black hair.

NOW ONE FOOT AND NOW THE OTHER. Tomi de Paola. G.P. Putnam's Sons. 1980.
When Grandfather suffered a stroke, Bobby teaches him how to walk just as his grandfather once taught him.

PATCHWORK QUILT. Valerie Flournoy. Dial Books for Young Readers. 1985.
Using scraps cut from the family's old clothing, Tany helps her grandma make a beautiful quilt that tells the many stories.

SONG AND DANCE MAN. Karen Ackerma. Scholastic. 1988.
Grandpa shares memories of his dancing days.

THINGS I LIKE ABOUT GRANDMA. Francine Haskins. Children's Book Press. 1992.
An African American girl recounts all the experiences she and her beloved grandmother share.

THUNDER CAKE. Patricia Polacco. (Philomel Books) Putnam Publishing Group. 1990
Through the wonderful tradition of baking a special "storm" cake, Grandmother helps rid her grandchild of the fear of thunderstorms.

THREE BRAVE WOMEN. C.L.G. Martin. Macmillian. 1991.
Mama and Grammy's humorous tales help Caitlin come to terms with her fear of spiders. This story deals with breaking the cycle of passing along fears to children.

A WALK IN THE RAIN. Ursel Scheffeler. G.P. putnam's Sons. 1986.

# ORDER FORM

Name_____
(Please print legibly)

Address _____

City _____ State _____ Zip _____

Please send me _____ copies of **Long Distance Grandparenting** at $7.95 per copy.

Shipping: Add $2.00 for the first copy and $.75 for each additional copy. (Allow 3-6 weeks for delivery)

Book(s)            _____
Shipping           _____
Tax (4% Michigan residents)    _____

Total  _____

**Send order to:**

Blanfield Publishing
P.O. Box 130316
Ann Arbor, Michigan 48113